PRAISE FOR *THE UNBELIEVING YELP OF PREY*

Poems that condemn a faith that failed the poet are legion. Poems that document a wrestling with the angel are rarer. Alex Mouw's *The Unbelieving Yelp of Prey* is a book of wrestling, not with faith so much as within faith, within the ideas we may or may not have about faith. In the tradition of Donne, these poems ascend and descend in an American idiom of hospital wards and Midwestern soybean fields, of Andy Warhol, NPR, and ASL. "Any hurt can be providence // if you wait long enough," Mouw writes, and he means to excavate the quiet wonder inside this recognition, where wonder takes the form not of blame, but of the kernel inside a question.

—G.C. WALDREP, author of *The Opening Ritual* and *The Earliest Witnesses*

"This isn't exactly a prayer," writes Alex Mouw at the start of this fine and theologically searching debut. In sonnets recalling Donne, Hopkins, Jarman, and Hill, Mouw wonders—in a world weighted down by suffering, how can we possibly pray? He concludes—as prey. In these poems, God is a hawk, a wolf, a dog with teeth bared; we are rabbits, voles, the smallest of the small. "I was afraid," Mouw writes, "and you baited me" and "So rarely do you have anything / to say that doesn't turn bloody." And yet, the speaker of these poems also yearns for God's presence, complaining, "I can't hold my need for you steady." Rooting down into the question of theodicy with Jobean stamina, Mouw pivots from desire to fear to anger and back again with a theological nimbleness that reminds me of Dickinson. In a world where God is weaponized, where the default mode seems to be prideful shouting instead of humble seeking, we need Alex Mouw's doubting and urgent voice. It is refreshing to see religious poetry this devastatingly human—which is to say, this deeply incarnate.

—MELISSA RANGE, author of *Scriptorium* and *Horse and Rider*

The Unbelieving Yelp of Prey bears witness to the manifold consequences of hunger and how it shapes our lives. In Alex Mouw's assiduous and ambitious debut collection, the pressure of hunger takes many shapes: restless faith, the body's intricate desires, and the mind's conflictual appetites for clarity and complexity. "Who would I bother if not my God, each / complaint and spinning holler pointed where?" begins the poem, "Apology for Belief," and I'm reminded that courage born of vulnerability is not so much a solution as it is crucial fuel to keep living, to keep going. These poems collage spiritual and bodily concerns through imagery born of Midwestern landscapes and mindscapes. They dwell in the tensions between wry humor, hurt, and something not quite akin to hope, where "faith pool(s)... like blood in a bruise." But I'm most impressed by how these poems balance wit and heart: Mouw's dynamic voice upends our expectations of what prayer can truly be.

—AARON COLEMAN, author of *Red Wilderness* and *Threat Come Close*

Like Gerard Manley Hopkins, Alex Mouw is God-driven, God-riven, and obsessed with the sonnet, a form that haunts this book. He details his disgruntlement with God's creation. An aunt becomes suicidal. A one-year-old's "trach tube, wider than a straw, wheezes." Through it all, Mouw plays his own music, "turns his favorite record up, the one // where the drummer beats the crash cymbal like / a captive who swears he doesn't know a thing." God is that drummer whaling on the world's crash cymbal. But listen to this captive poet. One might think of his book as a sonnet where doubt and unbelief occupy its octave, but with a *volta* or turn to moments of illumination—at dusk, the "surround- / sound drumming of bugs in every shadow tree." Mouw makes music out of the divine dissonance that surrounds him. His music mesmerizes, even as it sometimes terrifies.

—DONALD PLATT, author of *Tender Voyeur* and *Swansdown*

The UNBELIEVING YELP OF PREY

ALEX MOUW

The UNBELIEVING YELP OF PREY

poems

21st Century Poets, No. 45

TRP: THE UNIVERSITY PRESS OF SHSU
HUNTSVILLE, TEXAS 77341

Library of Congress Cataloging-in-Publication Data

Names: Mouw, Alex, 1992- author
Title: The unbelieving yelp of prey : poems / Alex Mouw.
Other titles: 21st century poets no. 45.
Description: First edition. | Huntsville : TRP: The University Press of SHSU, 2026. | Series: 21st century poets ; no. 45
Identifiers: LCCN 2025036510 (print) | LCCN 2025036511 (ebook) | ISBN 9781680034509 trade paperback | ISBN 9781680034516 ebook
Subjects: LCSH: Religious adherents--Michigan--Poetry | Belief and doubt--Poetry | LCGFT: Poetry | Religious poetry | Parodies (Literature)
Classification: LCC PS3613.O884 U53 2026 (print) | LCC PS3613.O884 (ebook)
LC record available at https://lccn.loc.gov/2025036510
LC ebook record available at https://lccn.loc.gov/2025036511

FIRST EDITION

Cover art: *In Mirror of Self* by Socorro Rico. Image courtesy of Nelson-Atkins Digital Production & Preservation, Gabe Hopkins.
Author photo by Emma Renaye Photography

Cover design by Cody Gates, Happenstance Type-O-Rama
Interior design by Maureen Forys, Happenstance Type-O-Rama

Printed and bound in the United States of America
First Edition Copyright: 2026

TRP: The University Press of SHSU
Huntsville, Texas 77341
texasreviewpress.org

CONTENTS

I

II

III

IV

For Stephanie

I

VESPERS IN THE MIDDLE OF NOWHERE

I drive, half-asleep, toward a stale hotel.
I'm inattentive, though not like a kid

engrossed in sci-fi novels
during math. Small-minded

like a rabbit in a garden
with no dog. In the twilight,

a Cooper's hawk, stiff and unblinking
on a farmer's fence. Voles tucked

in their catacombs. I enter a quiet
highway town, see the crosswalk

through which parents will guide
their children in the morning,

pulling coats tight and wincing
in headlights as a volunteer raises

her stop sign against the flow of traffic.
And the church door, red for tongue,

for spirit, a summons. This isn't
exactly a prayer. It's more

the unbelieving yelp of prey
grabbed suddenly by a wolf

that slipped, unnoticed, between
the trees. Behind the wheel,

I'm listening for a voice, honeyed
and jealous, to ask *where are you?*

DUALISM

Once, I begged my friends to let me
jump in a lake during an electric storm,
water shining like an obsidian door
when lightning clustered overhead.

I wanted to leap through. As a boy,
leaning over Saturday's oatmeal,
I told my father I would be a preacher.
That's hard work, he said. *Follows you*

wherever you go. It wasn't death
that made me give it up. It was the funeral
officiant who, corralling our weeping
family to the stiffened shape

in an open casket, called it Sally
or Hamilton as if it were still family.
I know it sounds desperate to think
of the soul as separate and possibly

immortal, but by the time my suicidal
aunt and cancerous, deflated
grandfather managed to rip away
from their own bones and sinews,

they'd earned the right to disappear
somewhere we wouldn't make a scene.

MY LORD I'VE FAILED AGAIN, GONE A WEEK

My Lord I've failed again, gone a week
without your presence—no statues or old trees
coming alive before my eyes, no slap
of light and wonder as I lean over

the bridge to watch brown and oiled water.
Master of the photon, of gluons, can you
make a gleaming breakfast plate or coffee
mug the start of understanding?

Of course you can, but what am I? Your goon
who searches books, riffles the pages like
a thousand doors whipping open then shut.
Who turns his favorite record up, the one

where the drummer beats the crash cymbal like
a captive who swears he doesn't know a thing.

WHITE EVANGELICAL, EARLY MILLENNIUM

We the scattered of Israel
here at Lake Michigan's weeping edge,
said the pastors of every Maranatha,
Park, and Harderwyk church.

They said, you are like a seed, small and frail.
They said, like a precious stone in a ring God wears

and I said, fill me to the brim. I waited
like the pews with delicately sawed scrollwork edges.

Once, the youth group strummed prayers for twenty-four hours.
That young woman's mother died anyway,
which called for different prayers.

Being a gift, faith pooled in me like blood in a bruise.
No matter how many times
I bowed at the altar, it ran
down my legs in cold blue boundary lines.

Being forced, it hardened wounds
to scars which keep a body together.

Our representatives prayed on television.
Our pastors prayed with hands on their shoulders.

We lived as if on a mountain crag.
We huddled as if besieged by Hittites.
The communion bread was sweet.

We read, The Everlasting
gathered you from dirt, His breeze
will blow you right back.
Sunning at the county beach in August

we dug in for rapture, armada
of leisure craft anchored on sand bars,
breakers straining them.

Elections in the narthex,
funerals and baptisms in the sanctuary,
wall-to-wall sheet cake in the basement after.
Any hurt can be providence

if you wait long enough.
Defeat can be persecution
if you believe in the LORD's rescuing arm.

Every week I lugged a guitar's
chipped sunburst, an amplifier's
scalding glass tubes to a church stage.

Calloused, my fingertips uncrackable
by steel strings, I looked over
the sea of mischief God and his people are.
I plucked our earthshaking hymns.

GUZZLE

On a sunken green couch in a mist
of wine and tears, you once said to me, "I wish that

someone would write my story" (the young dead sisters who test
your faith, the life of clawing debt), "that

I was recognized as brave. I tally anniversaries, pray for rest
whole nights awake, but no one seems to hear that."

At the time, I doubted there could be a novel for thirst
that drinks itself parch again, that

makes a puny fist. Now, years after my best
attempts to wave you off, I understand wanting all that

pain shaped to an arc, an uplifting toast
given in a banquet hall to applause so thick that

it heals real life. Do you remember how Christ
begged his Ancient of Days, "Will you take this cup from me?" Despite that

bloody crown and heaving chest,
the answer was a bitter, unspoken *no*. And though Christ screamed that

whole night, he never really tried to bust
the chains, stop the hurt. He reached for that

cup of pain which looked as endless as it felt pointless.
He drank as friends wordlessly fled. Who does that?

MY LORD IT WAS A COPPERHEAD WITH HER JAW

My Lord it was a copperhead with her jaw
unhinged, a hippo's watery pink gullet
made me think of you, how their hunger
swallowed things whole. A hundred penguins

scuttled after each other in colonies, bears
sunned outside their den, and three horses fenced
at the edge of the zoo stood still, eyeing
people as they left. Are you cool with all

those walls? The lion stretched like I do, in
yoga, palms planted and ass aimed heavenward.
A mother didn't stop her son's snow cone
flying through that fence. I tried to organize

a coup in the butterfly house but all they
wanted to do was drift from lilac to milkweed.

MY WIFE DOESN'T GET EITHER JOB

All the dust at home shifts a quarter inch
and she gnaws on chocolate chips,
contemplating survival

while upstairs in 3B
"Sweet Caroline" is playing
loud enough to make her eyes

soupier. She imagines a park
dotted with pastel balloons
which children eventually release,

and this makes her feel better
for thirty-eight seconds. All day
I've been hiding at the desk

tallying up my own stupid paychecks—
not enough. We should rent out
our bedroom. We should

see if eBay still exists and sell my copy
of *Grow Your Own Foliage*, sell
three wedding gift pillows emblazoned

HOME IS WHERE THE HEART IS.
If we could invite the richest owls
to our apartment and seek patronage

over my famous field game stew,
I'd be quite the provider. A cockroach
steps from the baseboard and shoos me

from his corner. I join my wife
at the window to see how slowly
Perseus and his star pals

drift. We put our foreheads
against the cold glass and watch
for what feels like a long time.

OR

Nettles thick as seminarian beards,
the pine trees knock heads
over the true nature of prophecy:
does God cause the people to be wicked
as an excuse to grind them down, or only
whisper the fact of wickedness?
The evergreens shake with that difficulty, dense
as the knots they can't cut off themselves.
What will take us to war: the president's hand
on a button (so I'm told apocalypse starts)
or a ban on icicle lights in Tunisia?
When do the meek start their shareholders' meeting?
Lord of hosts, rivet the gray sky to horizon—
so badly do we need containment.
The trees nod their assent and go on flailing,
hurling off loose branches, creaking
louder than the flagellated servants of Baal.
If not the hammer of hurricanes
or enormous bubbles of crude oil popped
and scattered over the face of the deep,
what's going to start the supplicant revolution?
Wind streams through the stand of trees
as through an enormous, forlorn oboe, whispering
You are to blame. Or you are not.
But you have nowhere else to go.

EXAMEN

You take memory like a wriggling sunfish
and you hold it to the light.
Note every spot and ridge, each scar
of hook. That's where God is,

the monk says to me. Prayer being neither
the coyote's ecstatic yip
nor the methodical cat running his grainy
tongue from shoulder to haunch.

My eyes close. My hands lie knuckle-down
on my thighs. *At the back of your mind*
do you see anything? No. *Good.*

What am I to do with anger?
Hold it up. It is an iron skillet warped from use
and crusted with burnt meat. The handle
is how you wield it. You must cradle it like a scalding
bowl or let it drop.

And disappointment? *Saltwater.*
Bathe, scrub your skin
like the flaking wallpaper it is, but do not drink.

What is a memory that consoles you?
Two trombones and a keyboard, a singer
kneeling at the guitar amp, her forehead
against the cabinet. *What moves*

through it? The microphone in her fist
loops a high squelch that flails a thousand watts
from rows of hanging speakers. The cup of wine
at the lip of the stage trembles.

The kick drum thrashes. The cup tips.
Cheap cabernet stains the plywood
and drips into the front row. *What does it mean to you?*

The taste of sour blackberry and oak. The guitar's last
wailing hook that dies amid a riot of applause.

MY LORD HOW PAINFUL IS SALVATION? IT'S

My Lord how painful is salvation? It's
against the rules to know but maybe so
are all my questions. Must I praise you
for my nerves twisted tight as shirt

hangers, fascia squeezing muscles
into atrophy—no doctor can tell
me why, no doctor smart as you.
If your surgery is sharp I fear for us

who make noisy work of our pain,
like children sucking on straws. Selfish
as a weed, I have to ask: am I damned
if I tell you Christ too often looks

too calm? Might I climb up, carve a frownier
mouth, something more, you know, human?

GOD IN A BOX

The preacher says God's love
is like the movie *Cars*.

This explains Christ's lesser-known miracle:
the oiling of the two thousand.

It's not that I don't like metaphors.
It's that when Christ lay down on a dead girl,

she woke to the smell of many days
in the desert, of stinking fish

and she wriggled under him, terrified.

For months she smelled him on everyone she knew

and when she heard the news,
that he'd marched out of his own grave, she asked

why would he do that?

Because love loses the race on purpose and the flashy
sports car learns his lesson, the preacher says.

Anyone in the congregation will tell you so.
The trees cracking in a storm will tell you so.

But the girl knew
that when Christ woke in pure dark
before folding the winding sheet
and shoving the tombstone aside

he felt the urge to lie back down,
leave the rest of us
to work things out.

II

DEATH DRIVE

Plotinus believed that inside him was a pelican
and that in its beak filled with steaming bathwater

he would prostrate, the long tongue rough against
his naked back as the bird took off. That's how

he planned to reach The One. What I've seen
is the body prone and discolored. A doctor

with her back discreetly turned. A plot of ground
bought mechanically. Without second thought

a steel excavator procured. My grandmother swore
heaven was an airport baggage claim she'd wander,

patiently peering out the dark windows until
grandfather found her. One night my widowed aunt

drove to a railroad crossing. Magnetized,
she stood up straight on the tracks, hands firmly

at her sides as the train unspooled towards her
like a reel of tragic film. Maybe after buckling up

in the flaming flying chariot, Elijah got lost
coursing Saturn's racetrack. My father wants

his body cast into Lake Michigan on an idling dinghy,
or to be cremated and scattered over his garden.

Whatever you do, he says, *don't bury me. No reason*
to hide the dead so shamefully underground.

MY LORD DESCEND FROM YOUR JUNGLE GYM

My Lord descend from your jungle gym
and observe those you've made. Kids wheel
in constant near-collision with each other
and every rusted metal shaft rising

blunt from dyed black mulch. A boy ducks
beneath a sagging chain-link bridge, tags
a girl's foot on the other side. She claws
up the slide, shoes slipping on plastic. Lord

I can't hold my need for you steady. It's
that old wooden game where the marble
wobbles through a maze dotted all over
with holes to fall through. And you wrench

yourself across the greasy rungs of monkey
bars. You perch atop the bright yellow slide.

IVAN KARAMAZOV'S CONFESSION

I told a roach he was ugly, even for his own
kind. Then four years of timber falling,
splitting inside my head. The moon is my
pillbox. I'm beating the walls of a humid
shack. The latch busted. A driver bobs atop
a carriage trundling across ruts. Amber light.
How could a grackle be responsible
for death by wagon wheel? Check with the garden
guitar player, the drunk sleeping in a snow bank.
I was on a train going east, counting
electric streetlamps as I went. My father
is dead. A voice told me so. It said *you*
did it. But I was out of town. I was a child
who leaves a ripped bit of his tongue
on a frozen ax head. I was an undigested
kernel of corn in the old man's last shit.

GEODE

—After a sculpture by Michael Ayrton

Miniature man of bronze, of thumbnail-sized head
crouched before a sheet of tinted glass,
can you see, behind the pane, the geode

you'll never touch? Left fist a perch for your chin,
right leg flung back like you're ready
to bolt—did you know that shell of quartz,

that meaty pyrite interior formed
inside a bubble of volcanic gas long before
either of us squatted to look? I learned that

just now, standing beside you with my phone.
In all your unblinking years, what have you learned
from the antediluvian whispers of rock?

Was the geode there when Charlemagne crossed
the Elbe? Has it heard Ezekiel
raving with sand in his mouth? I can step

clean past the translucent screen, revere
the geode's purple-veined brightness, its perfect
cleft the work of a diamond blade.

I can see everything you can't—landscapes, war
propaganda, a Japanese crucifix—my heels
the only sound on the museum floor. I watch you

from the geode's side of the wall, and I can barely
make out the map of your face: a small rise of lips, moat
of iris maybe. You might as well be anybody.

THOUGHTS AND PRAYERS

When I pray for justice, I see the backpack
a cop has torn from a young man shaken

over the sidewalk. To the open-mouthed delight
of the gathered crowd, not a gun, not a box of candy

presumed stolen, not even a stack of bootlegged
pornos falls out, but fifty apples that thud

against the ground before fathers and mothers
who lost their jobs assembling Ford power

windows. In my prayer the officer strips
to an undershirt permanently yellowed

with sweat. He drapes his blue jacket across
the man's shoulders like a soldered sheet

of bruises. God swoops from a pine tree,
skitters over the concrete, caws. My bird of prayer

needles its beak into one bright apple, digs up
the seeds and, with a backward tilt and squeeze

of its black gullet, sends them down to steep in bile.
All with a raging screech the crowd hears only as grief.

PSALM 139 FROM A DOWNTOWN WINDOW

If I flop in the reeking koi pond,
you are there. If I smother my thoughts
with rum, say "I will disappear
until morning," you are unyieldingly
awake. I once thought we were
pen pals and you'd keep my secrets,
intervene with job opportunities
and no-good girlfriends. That wasn't it.
I was afraid and you baited me
from my corner of sulk and coffee.
I grew ashamed and you covered me
in a woolen sweater. I know nil
about you but you're everywhere
and nowhere, so did you kill
all those grandparents, slick the roads
with ice and let kids live
in needling poverty? That would make
us enemies, which works for me
but for the rippled shine of a steelhead,
sunsets spilled like wine on a tablecloth,
the sound of awning vinyl snapped taut
in the wind. Beauty is a point
in your favor but no consolation against war,
etc. So rarely do you have anything
to say that doesn't turn bloody. I'm not
with you, I forgive you nothing, yet you
enwrap me like a fresh bandage tightly wound.

MY LORD WHO WAS IT YOU LAST SMOTE?

My Lord who was it you last smote?
Rockefeller, Jackson, Tupac, Plato?
If I were you I'd send Dostoyevsky's
ghost, onion breath and all, to rough up

consciences from Dayton to Siberia.
The homeless man I met today, reeking
of tobacco and sweat—if you put him
in bed beside me, breathing into my

mouth, I'd squirm and hog the sheets. I bought him
coffee, then pointed to the shelter five blocks
away, a squat brick barracks where tenants
shave and attend Bible study to earn

their beds. Wind off the river reached under
my flannel. It rippled his canvas jacket.

THE NINETEENTH CENTURY

is written in white capital letters at the top
of an oversized book, with Eugène Delacroix's
Liberty Leading the People on the cover.

The painting is cropped to Liberty's face
and bared breasts. There's a bayonet
just to the side of her which suggests, historically,

that a soldier who could have stabbed her
chose instead to cut down her dress.
That's the story of the century. Three or more

brightly colored French revolutions
are prelude to Russia in 1917, which is just
the opening credits to Cold War.

Napoleon versus Lenin—who would you
rather meet in an alley? At a bar? I am
too small to survive a revolution, a word

that actually means thousands of angry people,
some with guns and others with a guillotine.
A woman with her chest exposed

and people on either side of a barricade
staring in unspoken ceasefire.
There is no such thing as a century.

Only the swirl of cement and guns on television,
a stone gargoyle sitting on the stoop
of the abandoned house next door, sticking

its tongue out. There is morning dark
with black coffee and the reasonable
likelihood that the sun will rise.

And my dog curled on his bed
in the corner, watching silently
as I write. He takes up so little space.

PERSEUS BEHEADING MEDUSA

—After an engraving by Andre Racz

He is clearly thrilled by the hardness
of his bicep as he clutches the severed

head of a woman. Medusa, after all,
wanted nothing more than to be alone,

tended to occasionally by sisters who had
no use for great beauty. Her face explodes

like a bloom of hydrangea, her pain
wild enough to seem monstrous.

In this story, a man seeks a woman
to give his own ugliness a face.

He kills her, and despite the soft body
on the ground, he sees himself

as the dutiful son of good men,
wiping his blade in the unkept grass.

MY LORD I SAW A DOG TODAY, AND SHE

My Lord I saw a dog today, and she
stood like a compass needle beside
her person—muscles tough as knotted
wood, thick grey fur, eyes shining. The harness

around belly and shoulders let the man
pull her from lunges at squirrels and finches,
the dark gurgling in her throat. She fell back
in line. Who bred the wolf out of her? Does

she know her incisors are sharp enough
to rip the throat of the man holding her back?
She knows nothing but dry food and his hands.
How pretty she looked with that blue leash. When

he let the line go slack, she turned to snap
at it like a wasp, caught his eye, turned back.

ARGUMENT WITH ORTHOPEDICS

I just want to fix people's limbs, Luke says
when I ask about the purpose of his residency,
and the word *just* rings like a finishing nail
hammered against concrete. It's evening, no
streetlights in Ann Arbor, Michigan where
we sit together for the first time since college.
We drink beer until we're immune to its smell
settling like fog on the screened-in porch. I ask
if he wonders about the limits of his trade,
the ignorance hemming his bleached coat
of expertise? *Believing you know it all,*
he says as the maple leans to one side
in open-armed compliance with the wind,
is how you survive a twenty-four-hour shift.
Earlier today he led me through the hospital,
floor after floor of dim labs and gleaming operating rooms.
Beside the man in a stained white apron
swiping cards at the cafeteria door, a nude sculpture
hunched with mendicant hands outstretched.
Patients touch its head for good luck, Luke said,
pausing like a docent before he led us on.
Down the hall, a hand-illuminated Bible lay open
under glass, and a monkey in the margin
reached to place an *o* in the gospel where a monk,
his wrists frayed by weeks of careful work,
had missed it. Last winter my own limbs were cut open
by a surgeon forty years Luke's senior.
I remember that doctor said, *ten percent chance*
we make things worse, and I remember
he arrived late to all our appointments, then rose

from his chair without answering my questions.
On the morning of surgery, he asked my permission
to pray, petitioned for steady hands
that I might move without pain again.
Moments later I was under. In this twilight,
Luke's eyes, wide and dark, make him look too young
for surgery. My nerves crackle—*probably permanent,*
the doctor said, *but anything can happen*.
The yard teems with fireflies. A racoon's shadow
climbs the fence. Luke gets up, passes into the kitchen
for another drink, then returns and confesses
that his days are boring: body after body
and their numbing rehearsal of symptoms,
prescriptions already given by a textbook. *It's hard,*
I say. *I needed six doctors to get an imperfect*
diagnosis. He replies, *what we think we feel*
and what's real rarely fit. I spend whole days
listening to patients, then I come home to study
what they mean. The night passes from dull
steel to pitch, and maybe it's a mercy
we can't see one another's faces. Rain begins
to fall on the porch roof, and every drop slaps
the corrugated metal with a fresh complaint.

III

A MORNING'S WORK

I'll be sitting, imagining myself reading a book
when, in deference to the sun rising like dough

just above the buildings, the streetlight outside
my window clicks off, suddenly reduced

to a translucent bubble full of cobwebs
and dead beetles. Imagine discovering anew

your own irrelevance each morning
when the world lights up without you,

and there are miles, continents, eons
you'll never know because you are so small.

When I sit in the same chair for hours
and see an office tower's gray capstone

etched HUIZENGA 1919, sometimes
I wonder about that. A truck,

a sports car, a cyclist speed toward
the day's goal, and two women run

on the sidewalk, the muscles of their legs
as well-defined as maps. The smell of ground

coffee and apple cider donuts, a rare
smoker hiding in an alley. I watch

as if that were my purpose on earth,
to be a tiny point of gravity. As if

observation could hold things together,
a landscape painting protect a real marsh.

The streetlight can't help me see, though
it is lit up again, not from within,

but by the sun passing through it, obscuring
its stains. It glows, like everything else

without fire or electricity, in light flung
towards us as a gift. Imagine not deserving

whatever warmth you've received.
Imagine being unable to give thanks.

GENESIS 3

After crocodiles lumbered off the shaven toenails
of the Word, after the most manic thought
became all birds. After the oceans
were put to bed and the sun

and stars sorted out their choreography.
After the after of time's trap door burst open
and covered the earth in wind—what?

A viral rot that spread like crazy?
You call it sin sometimes, which is,

without ever knowing what exactly,
knowing utterly that you are wrong
at a depth you can't, finally, know.

After that, the blinds all snap upwards,
retreating to scrolls in their high, plastic cases.
Brightness enters the room as a raiding party.
This has answered no questions, so you wait

within a silence rich as the hollow
of an unbowed cello. It continues to snow,
which you think deserves to be part of any

abject falling into sin, but is only
a northern add-on. Plows are piling it up.
This is how exile feels:

an acoustic guitar
played so softly you can hear

the thumb pad dragged across the string
as it releases a barely plucked note.
The scratch of metal and the middle C

between which almost no one would distinguish.
Yet one is music; the other, cold mechanics.
Where is this going? The chapter just ends

with a flaming sword spinning like a windmill.
It must have been gorgeous from far away.

MY LORD I SIT BEIGE AND BUBBLE-WRAPPED

My Lord I sit beige and bubble-wrapped
when all my friends forsake me for jobs
in California, Illinois, Texas. When I hear
one of them got a new car, a shepherd

puppy with ears like full sails, I want to
fly to Vienna again, eat fried pork
each night and wander the hills at the edge
of town until I find the lean-to

where, years ago, I sat with my teacher,
the city lights spread like a picnic blanket
beneath us. He drank till he was blubbering
that Augustine was the most beautiful man

in history: *God flowing through each word*
like whitewater rapids. Can you imagine?

AUBADE AS PREY

A mourning dove does its tragic morning thing
not outside the window to my left,
where I could watch the alto swelling in its chest,
but westward, behind me, through the apartment's brick wall.
She startles me like the preacher does,
sometimes, booming from the church stage
Who is it that you're looking for?
yet raising the hairs of my neck like a whisper.
I swivel my head to blankness.
The sky is gray as distant lake water and the sound
has slipped in me like fishing line.

STILL LIFE WITH MARRIAGE

Prostrate on top of the sheets, I feel lacquered nails
bloom from my tailbone. For every inch
she scratches, another inch wakes, suddenly
parched. She rounds my hips, returns
to center spine, her fingers stretched to cover

as much of me as possible. Because I am not
an athlete, not skilled in trapping or farming,
it's remarkable that she treats my body as if it's worth
preserving, like leather she sets her nose against,
the faint smell of sweat proving it's broken in

and can take more use. This isn't just the pleasure
of being touched near midnight. It's not beauty, either—
any painter would note the holes in my ratty
shorts, her face chapped from washing.
It's like a dog who barked at the window all day

and lunged for every acorn on the sidewalk,
now happily entering a crate. Just as he's drawing
into himself, a hand reaches through the bars,
cornbread under the fingernails, and he shivers
from his rest—head down, mouth open.

ECSTATIC

—Antony Gormley. Untitled (for Francis).
Lead, fiberglass, and plaster

A seam splits Francis down the front.
Jagged wounds perforate his hands, feet,
and chest. *The artist does not want to identify*

the figure with a particular religion, according
to the curator's plaque. Francis accepts
the uniformly stale museum light open-handed,

egg-smooth head upturned, sexless crotch wide-set
and braced. Who needs cheekbones when visited
by a god without particulars? The other tourists

wind around me wearing floral joggers
and off-kilter Yankees caps. They skip Francis
and go on to Warhol's glossy colors and a great

glass disc, strung up in the center of the room,
which sprays diffracted light across the walls. Is Francis
just ugly? Soldered lead across the shoulders and waist

slices him like a butcher's diagram, exactly
ridiculous enough to be holy. Francis, do you like
standing pierced and thrilled while rivers of people

ignore you? What is it that stuffs you full of sugar
and nails? Do you even know what you're doing
here? Please please shake your head yes or no.

A SCIENTIST ON THE BBC EXPLAINS ELECTROMAGNETISM

Obvious, really. It requires
no advanced knowledge
to see everything
is, deep down, electric.
You learned it
same as I did, grade
school: an overhead
projector shining both
waves and particles
on a dirty screen,
a transparency worksheet
demonstrating the absolute
minutia of atoms made
of charges wrenched or
clinging like wet mint
to the side of a cocktail
glass. The tiniest
constituents of matter
are charged, yet we touch
our bedsheets, tires,
paper on the table
without shock. Beyond
the smallness a microscope
can reach, we detect
a heaving, perfectly
matched contest of protons
and quarks that prevents
lightning in fresh coffee
for no reason we can see.
Still we peer from the dark

as into the lit interior
of an apartment
owned by a stranger
whose wealth and taste
in furniture we
can't yet fathom.

MY LORD I'M NOT TOO FAR GONE, RIGHT? SURE

My Lord I'm not too far gone, right? Sure
I live some nights on the manic edge
but never howled, delusional, through town.
I don't infidel my wife, I keep the beer tamed—

maybe everyone stokes with their
personal bellows the sulking fire of
no one understands me. Even this
poem, I want to know if you like it, if

it's worthy. At a ceramics studio
I saw a novice work a new form, pull
a plate from the wet clay ball, dimple the edge
and scratch circles in the center. Then she smashed

it. *Ten thousand before I can fire one*. So,
Lord, whom did you make and break today?

NPR'S SCIENCE FRIDAY AT THE INTERSECTION OF GRANT AND 24TH

Seconds after the Big Bang, the universe
entered a Dark Age—prior to

and not to be confused with
medieval indulgence sellers,
whole lives used copying Pentateuchs—

and for millions of centuries,
nothing, says the radio scientist.
Even to call it dark is too cozy.

And I thought today was important,
traffic slow as honey.

And ninety-seven percent of the universe
is plasma? asks the interviewer.

In a way, answers the scientist. But
if you flip every person, gadget
and meal inside-out, perceive them
from all angles at once,

there's another form of matter,
entirely different and,
well, unobservable.

Outside my car, finches
peck a styrofoam plate of Chinese takeout.
A crow shivers, flattens its wings.

The scientist continues: we guess at dark matter
by the way stars flow through space
with the precision of a waiter

pouring wine. But it refuses
to stand still or be measured.
A group of students passes

on a crosswalk, a woman with feather earrings
and a man who cut off
the bottom halves of his denim pant legs.

I see a beer can
crushed to a wide coin,
something an ancient human

might spend on seeds, on weapons,
and were he gangrenous
or soaked with flu and chills,

on the quick alto notes
of an icaro, his head tilted back
as the shaman drips a bright
green potion into his waiting mouth.

MY LORD WHEN YOU FOLD A SOUL TO YOURSELF

My Lord when you fold a soul to yourself,
do you make of it an origami crane?
Does it hurt to crease all those sharp angles
and lines? Did Aunt Sally believe she was

wrapped in another depression before she
looked full in your face, scarred as ancient
marble, bright as a house fire? What are
our first words to you? *Careful, Please, Not yet?*

Enough questions. I submit myself for
consideration, without much confidence,
for a seat at your table. Don't answer yet.
I'll keep half an eye angled on headlights

of oncoming trucks, the spider web on
my lintel. Let me know when you're ready.

IV

ILLUMINATION

Yet another sun rises like an incandescent lemon,
and my attention is a thick shirt slung
over a drying rack. Lord
make me better, by which I mean less bored.

At this moment ants heave brick
dust to and fro as they construct the sacred dome
of their living, and a rabbit bolts

from a sudden noise, her ears aligned
more precisely than the downhill skis of an Olympian.
If I'm as straightforwardly chemical

as the buzzing air conditioner, I should fuss
less, like the pallid sturgeon that skim rivers

from Montana to New Orleans and ply for food
with their needle noses, ancient and mute
beneath the water's surface.

Who made this mind to pout and marvel
and tell you its every bend in thought? Make me

a sturgeon: threatened by extinction,
without panic I'd haunt the lower currents,
hungry even when I slept.

MY LORD HOW DO YOU BUILD A LAKE? HOW LONG

—St. John's Abbey

My Lord how do you build a lake? How long
did it take to hollow this plain of red clay
and funnel rain into Lake Sagatagan?
The monks only swim here with the abbot's

dispensation, but the complaints of
mourning doves and blackbirds, the loon's anxious
rippling *o*, the drunk looping of turkey
vultures—these start in the morning to set

the day's metronome ticking. Then humidity
spikes by noon in plodding, sticky quatrains
which are reliable, though unrhymed. Then
the sun turns its last click into the water,

a tarp lifts off the stars, up starts surround-
sound drumming of bugs in every shadow tree.

IN THEIR OWN IMAGE

One mile from the concrete Bauhaus cathedral, down
a trail crisscrossed with roots and fallen birches,

stands an empty chapel dedicated to Mary. We enter
the thin painted door to huge spiders, black and brown,

pocked with bits of white and yellow, each waiting
for the moth wobbling around the rim of the ceiling light.

Hilary arrived before us. She's sitting in the only chair
on the mosaic floor. While she is here on leave,

her husband remains in Texas with their year-old son,
who's watching American Sign Language on a computer screen,

whose trach tube, wider than a straw, wheezes. His
working eye scans the colored spines of his mother's

books. He drums with a toy horse on an empty soup bowl,
on the tub's claw foot. He will have another surgery when she

gets back. We ask why the wooden icon of Mary looks so
out of proportion, and Hilary tells us the monks make each one

in their own image. Some have sharp angles, as though
their makers' prayers were hard. See, she says,

see how this one's tiny eyes were gouged from the wood,
hooded by her brow. See her chest like split honeycomb.

PSALM 43 DRIVING THROUGH THE HEARTLAND

Mind the red-tailed hawk
who waits on the green rim
of an interstate exit sign,
scanning the landscape: when
grass rustles with the slightness
of a mouse or rabbit, she
is not casual. No carrion content
to glide in sloping circles,
she flaps like a freestyle swimmer
and dives at a steep angle,
talons outstretched. Consider
the mole, who lifts his head
just above ground and cannot tell
if it is only the sun bearing
down on him, or the whistling
approach of a predator.
Why are you doubled over,
oh my soul? And why so
limp within me? The leaves
float like small canoes
for your pleasure, the last snow
dissolves beneath your boots.
The dirt softens each March
beneath warm scat,
preparing to welcome all things.
Hope in God, for he will see
the landfill covered in grass
like a funereal mound. He will
sweep you up for what you are: prey,
blind and hungry, searching the air.

APOLOGY FOR BELIEF

Who would I bother if not my God, each
complaint and spinning holler pointed where?
I've tried groveling before birds, beseeched
my laptop's kernel threads for a better,
less mixed-up world. My wife, yes, she loves me
and is human. Mom and dad similar,
but they first weighted me with piety,
Jesus baggage. I tell my familiars
everything but need to scream my head off
in a Bible cocoon so tightly bound
it passes for love, so sharp it can slough
entire selves. Dimly lit, a shrink once found
I should love myself. Who'd pierce me? I thought.
Who would lure me through depths and not be caught.

A SHORT CATALOG OF MIRACLES

It was not my idea that water should bead and roll off
the mandarin duck, his cinnamon and crimson feathers
seeming to leap from the algae-dull surface of the pond.
Neither am I responsible for the tablet computer
which calculates a waiter's tip with uncharitable
precision. Once I drank too much wine and babbled
the shame I feel for carting flowers to local shows
and presenting them to a cellist who, despite my
near-prayerful begging over many tasteless meals,
did not love me. In this way I am like God, who
does not command so much as chase the sun, which is
always spinning off as if toward the dark corner of a
crowded dance floor. It's a wonder I didn't carry around
an electric keyboard to fill my life with the grand
and tragic piano riffs of a rock opera. That I stumbled
on a love flourishing as carelessly as a petunia.
On paydays we buy sushi—even when one of us is out
of a job—we can hardly stand how rich and hungry
we feel. Sometimes I walk to the small lake down the road
and watch the heron standing in the swamp,
left leg poised in front of the right, wings half-raised
and crimped, ready to spring who knows exactly when.

OBLITERATE

Not dust, not torqued steel pipe or car doors
littered like shields across a landfill. Bones

look strangely permanent, abstracted as they are
from the given man or dog. *Nothing really*

disappears, says the expert physicist, his bald
head shiny as a crystal ball: *eventually it's converted*,

made a new phase of matter. Even a father's cup
so affectionately filled with vodka and pear,

topped with basil? Ashes spread across water?
What if our dead don't rot at all? If what happens

is electric, a current hauling across town. Just
as a rotted tree branch cuts the line, sparks leap

into the air without passion to join the diffuse
light of the evening streetlamps. Then they're gone.

MY LORD, YES, HI, COULD YOU PUT G.M. HOPKINS

My Lord, yes, hi, could you put G.M. Hopkins
on the line? On the subject of praise
I have a question: if a rainbow fits
over woods like a heaven-tent, or say

the stars seem extra lit up with gossip
about how gorgeous still water is, and
no one on earth says anything, are we
a disappointment? Does God wish we'd trip

over curbs or stray footballs, calling out
root, turd, cleft bean? Does G.M. miss it here?
I drove ten hours through fields yesterday and
think it would've floored him: how 80 mph smears

acres of soybeans, a man fixing his bike,
a sign for corn to one green streak.

WEDDING PIANIST

At dinner, when someone calls for Michael Jackson
or Bach or Rihanna, he thinks the key, hears the melody,
then splays his hands again in origami twists
across the five-octave Yamaha. Half the guests

can't tell he sprinkles ad-libbed blues solos,
he sounds so radio. A dozen encircle his corner of gear,
doe-eyed because he has no sheet music
and—according to the father of the bride—he can't

even read treble clef. We used to play together
in bars and megachurches. Between sets
he asked if I still gigged. No—that dazzle
of augmented chords, dominant suspended flowing

from the same twelve notes long since
lost me. Across the ballroom he pauses, hands
loose above the keys. He begins the piece
he wrote for the first dance, something

that coils and springs with a pop riff, rages
with the wide bass chords of a hymn. His hands fly
bright red and mixolydian as he nods half out of time,
grinning, eyes fixed nowhere, not of this world.

LAST ADDRESS TO THE LORD

What did you mean when   you opened

the book

with a spider crushed

between its pages
and said

eat these words?

What did you mean

when your lips brushed mine
your mouth like an untapped oil well?

I am trying to reach you still.

See how trees   keep even their dead
leaves   in an orbit

around themselves?

Why don't you
pull close what falls away?

Sick with waiting
I checked the lake

even stirred

the water with a cattail   made beautiful

ripples that were not   forthcoming
                                         found termites
in a maple

                              but never you

      so I looked

in the asthmatic shaft   of the chimney

and thought I heard a whisper   the wind

      probably   in the dark
                              capped at the top.

I wanted to call out
            scream something needy

crouched with my head torqued in

                  that darkness was so thick

it wrapped me up   like nothing.

INCARNATE

This morning's light looks chalky, a dusting
from on high or else the airborne rubble
of distant desert cities where screeching
planes mean *hide*. Astride, weepy amid all
this trouble—Christ in a breastplate of bark,
raiment of leaves whooshing laps around him.
I might shit myself in fear as a dark
wail blooms from his mouth. His awful cries rim
the earth and tear me in dissonance. Why
show up to all this nonsense? His wounds pour
sap, sweet and unrefined and I might die
of holiness. Christ offers bread to poor
coma patients, arms endangered blossoms
with petals. Just how did I think he'd come?

ACKNOWLEDGMENTS

My great thanks to the editors of publications in which these poems appear or are forthcoming, sometimes with alterations:

America: "Apology for Belief"

Briar Cliff Review: "Thoughts and Prayers"

Christianity and Literature: "God in a Box"

Cider Press Review: "In Their Own Image"

The Colorado Review: "My Lord how do you build a lake? How long" and "My Wife Doesn't Get Either Job"

The Dalhousie Review: "Death Drive" and "Examen"

December: "A Morning's Work," "A Scientist on the BBC Explains Electromagnetism," and "Obliterate"

descant: "Ecstatic"

The Evansville Review: "Dualism"

The Florida Review: "My Lord who was it you last smote?"

Jet Fuel Review: "My Lord how painful is salvation? It's" and "My Lord I'm not too far gone, right? Sure"

Grain: "A Short Catalog of Miracles" and "Wedding Pianist"

The Los Angeles Review: "My Lord I saw a dog today, and she"

The Minnesota Review: "Perseus Beheading Medusa"

North American Review: "Aubade as Prey"

Peatsmoke: "Geode"

Phoebe: "Illumination"

Quarter After Eight: "Last Address to the Lord," "Or," and "Psalm 139 from a Downtown Window"

Rhino: "Genesis 3"

Ruminate: "NPR's Science Friday at the Intersection of Grant and 24th"

Southern Indiana Review: "My Lord I've failed again, gone a week" and "My Lord, yes, hi, could you put G.M. Hopkins"

The Southern Review: "Vespers in the Middle of Nowhere"

Southword: "Ivan Karamazov's Confession"

Tahoma Literary Review: "The Nineteenth Century"

Tupelo Quarterly: "Argument with Orthopedics"

Typehouse Literary Magazine: "My Lord it was a copperhead with her jaw" and "My Lord when you fold a soul to yourself"

West Branch: "Incarnate"

Thanks to the humane and ambitious role models who have taught me, among them Jack Ridl, Heather Sellers, Donald Platt, and Marianne Boruch. Thanks also to the friends who helped shape this book, especially Bess Cooley, Lauren Mallett, Anthony Sutton, and Derick Mattern. Thanks to J. Bruce Fuller and the folks at TRP for being energetic champions. Thanks to my parents, who made the mistake of sending me to a local poetry workshop as a teen. Most of all, thanks to Stephanie, whose support makes writing possible and worth doing.

ABOUT THE AUTHOR

ALEX MOUW is an assistant professor of English at Samford University. His poetry and scholarship appear in *The Southern Review*, *The Massachusetts Review*, *Twentieth-Century Literature*, and elsewhere. He lives with his wife and two children in Birmingham, Alabama.

21ST CENTURY POETS

21st Century Poets is a collection of full-length poetry books by TRP authors whose first book of poetry was released after the year 2000.

BOOKS IN THIS SERIES:

No. 001 — Kendall Dunkelberg — *Time Capsules*

No. 002 — William Bedford Clark — *Blue Norther and Other Poems*

No. 003 — Karla K. Morton — *Names We've Never Known*

No. 004 — Ben Greer — *The Bright House*

No. 005 — Beryl Lawn — *Poems from Both Sides of the Fence*

No. 006 — Swep Lovitt — *Sometimes the World Is Too Beautiful*

No. 007 — William Wright — *Bledsoe*

No. 008 — Sarah Cortez — *Walking Home*

No. 009 — Jesse Graves — *Tennessee Landscape with Blighted Pine*

No. 010 — Richard Boada — *The Error of Nostalgia*

No. 011 — Sarah Cortez — *Cold Blue Steel*

No. 012 — David Havird — *Map Home*

No. 013 — Beryl Lawn — *More Poems from Both Sides of the Fence*

No. 014 — Jesse Graves — *Basin Ghosts*

No. 015 — Karla K. Morton — *A Constant State of Leaping*

No. 016 — Kendall Dunkelberg — *Barrier Island Suite*

No. 017 — Stephen Gibson — *The Garden of Earthly Delights*

No. 018 — Karla K. Morton — *Accidental Origami: New and Selected Works*

No. 019 — Karla K. Morton — *Wooden Lions*

No. 020 — Mary Morris — *Enter Water, Swimmer*

No. 021 — Elisabeth Murawski — *Heiress*

No. 022 — Randall Watson — *The Geometry of Wishes*

No. 023—Sarah Kain Gutowski—*Fabulous Beast*

No. 024—Jennifer Sperry Steinorth—*A Wake with Nine Shades*

No. 025—Mary Morris—*Dear October*

No. 026—Andrew Hemmert—*Sawgrass Sky*

No. 027—Matt W. Miller—*Tender the River*

No. 028—Jesse Graves—*Tennessee Landscape with Blighted Pine* (10th Anniversary Edition)

No. 029—Forrest Rapier—*As the Den Burns*

No. 030—Sarah Audsley—*Landlock X*

No. 031—Luke Johnson—*Quiver*

No. 032—Sarah Kain Gutowski—*The Familiar*

No. 033—Joshua Robbins—*Eschatology in Crayon Wax*

No. 034—Theodora Ziolkowski—*Ghostlit*

No. 035—Kimberly Ann Priest—*tether & lung*

No. 036—Mary Morris—*Lanterns in the Night Market*

No. 037—Daniel Lassell—*Frame Inside a Frame*

No. 038—Luke Johnson—*Distributary*

No. 039—Brooke Sahni—*In This Distance*

No. 040—Randall James Tyrone—*City of Dis*

No. 041—Ryan Vine—*The Cave*

No. 042—Aaron Baker—*American Experiment*

No. 043—Lauren Camp—*Is Is Enough*

No. 044—Donovan McAbee—*Holy the Body*

No. 045—Alex Mouw—*The Unbelieving Yelp of Prey*

No. 046—Remi Recchia—*Addiction Apocalypse*